ELIZABETHAN

X

JONATHAN LOVEJOY

Jonathan Lovejoy

ELIZABETHAN

The Complete Poems of Elizabeth Peele

Volume X

Jonathan Lovejoy

✝ Armageddon Publishing

Cover: *Elegy*, 1899
William Adolphe Bouguereau (1825-1905)

ISBN-10: 0692331999
ISBN-13: 978-0692331996

For every Elizabeth

Introduction

Carmen Angelina Coletti (Elizabeth Peele) was perhaps the greatest composer who ever lived. After her death, studies of her music revealed a body of work—almost exclusively instrumental—of such beauty and power as to defy description. Even so, her lifelong reclusiveness rendered them obsolete to the world, and these musical treasures may remain apart from public view forever.

Even those few who heard her original scores did so in quiet apprehension, that this beautiful widow—lost somewhere deep in North Carolina farming country—brought forth music as completely ingenious as any ever written before. The sounds of greatness flowing from this woman's piano, surely this is not meant to be! For what purpose can she truly serve as a neoclassical composer in a jaded modern world, except as a curiosity and eventually, a fountain of eternal exploitation?

But while music did serve as a profession for her since she was twelve—her only wage being a sound mind and spirit—there was still another expression, both private and unintentional, equally meant for her eyes only. Gathered posthumously, so few of these "assemblies" can be called unique or special, and likely cannot set her apart from any other lonely poet in the world. But still they live on, as a glimpse into the mind of a musical genius and abused woman of Faith. Written parallel to her music over the years—with no striving for greatness or immortality—these poetic trifles, ironically, may be the only compositions of hers the world will ever hear.

Jonathan Lovejoy

ELIZABETHAN

or

"The Assemblies"

Volume X

Jonathan Lovejoy

Elizabethan X

Such is the grandest music among us—

Poets...

Such are the wildest thoughts among us—

Composers...

The Book of Simone

298th Assembly

1337

*T*he earth is the devil's domain

The first heaven is his

Principalities and powers

Ruling the clouds of spring

Satan dances a moonlit night

Above the prairie green

Wishing for my annihilation

But being unable

1338

As to the ghost which torments him

She screams a bloody rake

Scraping nerves with merely a voice

To shake the dead awake

The ghost is in the photograph

For dying eyes to make

1339

Oh, such grand delusions are they

What grand illusions may

Torment the heart and mind with hope

For such things never stay

Oh, 'tis a home for living in

This place we've never been

Rolling above our horizon

In His due time again

299th Assembly

1340

Bald-headed bastard

Abusing your kid

Going to Hell faster

'Cause of what you did

Arrogance has resonance and dissonance in your soul

When the pressures of your life take hold—

And you fold your hand over your three year old daughter's neck and squeeze

Until the bubbles gurgle in her throat

Bald-headed bastard—

Abusing your kid—

Going to Hell faster—

'Cause of what you did

1341

Lightning strikes in a minor key

Outside the learning hall

Hands carved out of the Dead Wood Tree

In prayer—one—and for all

Jonathan Lovejoy

1342

What mountainous beauty I surmise!
Heavy from such glory—there be
Booming—crashing waves of power
Such to bring me to my knees

Would that the artist's feather quill
Had blessed unskillful hands
As too, desired sculptor's blade
To carve thine immortality

By a Divine hand alone
Doth such wonders be
A reduction to tears and quivering
The rest of humanity

What mountainous beauty in disguise!
Fettered by the cloth to carry
Thy burden—heavy in desire
To flame a fire in my soul

Elizabethan X

There, bombs burst thy sweetness through

To capture a heart in agony

Though in innocence, Creation sings

Thy mountainous infinity

1343

*E*very morning—when I awake

I am risen from the dead

300th Assembly

Jonathan Lovejoy

1344

Roll the poison out with a stick

'Til it be twisted gone

Harvest the field that is grown in

Though it be past the time

When the poison is rolled away

A healing can begin

Strength to nourish the harvest field

And promises therein

1345

The dough rises into profit

But for a chosen few

The rest labour disolutioned

In bondage to their greed

Wealth and riches bestow at birth

Seed planted in the mud

Growing from soil enriched with life

Protected from the flood

1346

Poverty crawls across the floor

Echoing in the room

Days of fear and sorrow

Do threaten to return

To breach the core of sanity

Uncleanliness to bear

Winds from the storm of poverty

Still blowing breezes there

A ghost from the house of shadows

Brings misery anew

That every life must bear the next

Comeuppance overdue

1347

'Tis a lack of understanding
For where such perversions be
Let them take your deposition
Before you go to jail

As surely as the world is round
Your precious day would come
To be the one thrown behind bars
For some untidy sum

The tiniest amount given
For the purpose of sin
In epic humiliation
Because of where you've been

Jonathan Lovejoy

301st Assembly

1348

The Maestro sings a happy tune
From 1823
Semiramide on the world stage
'Til the end of the earthen age

Turning the page of history
Burning for all to see

The Maestro sings a happy tune
In 1823
Semiramide on the world stage
For everyone to see

1349

Misery is of little import
Nor a desired trait
Close the gate on her company—
When she comes to call!

There's no need to voice everything
Thy speech to pick and choose
Lest their ears do rattle and hum
As eyes go drift to snooze

Wake up! Get up!
Clean up! Shape up!
Go carnival the cruise
Roll away from the rock bottom
There's nothing more to lose!

1350

The beds are made—
The plans are laid—
The fields are rich and green
But every ear of corn there 'bouts
Is flavored of leaf and lean

Done with sackcloth and ashes!
None spin time the faster!
Rather yet serve the Lord thy God
And Christ thy Lord and Master!

No suffering—fast or bitter prayer
Can bring the harvest soon
So rest thy head in thine grieving bed
And contemplate a tune

1351

Exposed breasts and marmalade fingers

What unholy good are they?

Will I. Am said it best

Whacha gon' do with all that breast?

In service to the road I fly

Rounding the nearest curve to die

To seek prosperity--bye and bye

With no tears left to cry

Hope dies at a moment's notice

With a broom handle in your hand

Use it--don't abuse it--

I know you didn't choose it--

But your bones will bleach anyway in the sand!

Jonathan Lovejoy

25

302nd Assembly

Jonathan Lovejoy

1352

If you have the proper look
You'll go far in life
Be it a handsome husband—
Or perhaps a pretty wife

What is it that you're doing here?
The one in charge will say
If you don't have the proper look
You'll be escorted away

1353

Look at that big valley when it manifests

Said the mother to her son

The boy nodded his head in revelation

Then showered 'til it was done

1354

Hoping for glass blown in wisdom
To appear in respective key
So that questions may be answered
Concerning prosperity

The hills have no remorse
Dying just the same
Keeping silent to watch you drown
In the Aftermath of Rain

1355

On racial sensitivity

The new norm—it is such

Racism is a wound healed over—

But painful to the touch

Jonathan Lovejoy

303rd Assembly

1356

The iron curtain—

Is not the steel curtain

Of Pittsburgh

Nor the Union of Soviet Socialist Republics

The Iron Curtain is Dorothy Hamill's haircut

From the 1970's

Vanity—

Forged in Iron and Steel

1357

Toss the aspirin into the woods

If it be layered "sick"

See the black line trajectory

Nearby the forest trees

Play the big game as it is dealt

Drive to the hoop you see

With no worries of its outcome

For loss or victory

1358

Hear the call of the whistling wind
Moan the pain of a thousand years
In one single breath

Obey the voice of the whistling wind
Seek shelter from the coming eschatology
The deluge of fire and blood
Smoke—rising from the rubble
Of future calamities unknown

Obey the voice of the rising wind
Flee the wrath to come!
The Earth rumbles in tune—
To the Call of the Whistling Wind

From the Garden of Antiquity
To the Garden of Gethsemane
From the Cross of Calvary
To eternity

1359

Apart the V shape in the sky
There flies a lonely goose
Upon wings of destination
So likewise as the V

Content to ride the wind alone
One shore to the other
Having learned by necessity
The company of one

What motivation is the V?
Of this, he cannot tell
Knowing he'd rather fly alone—
Or die and go to Hell

Jonathan Lovejoy

304th Assembly

1360

Suffer the rose colored dawn

If flows the window of spring

From the gate across the prairie green

The morning light is shown

1361

The wind whistles of my demise

On early Spring and sunny skies

In whirling all around—

Though I endeavor not to hear

The moaning of the wind is clear:

"Here lies your burial mound!"

1362

$\mathcal{M}$aking me endure her beauty by power
Could I suffer the strain?
Married to a timeless Beauty
By an Italian name

To all of her friends--a wedding
"I'm getting married," she would say
In love with the groom's attractiveness
And the diamond engagement ring

1363

*T*he wise speaks silly hazes of demure—

In the prison of broken dreams

Jonathan Lovejoy

305th Assembly

1364

I sing a song of weariness

Burned into the wood

A testament to tiredness

Inspired as it should

A Melody for The Lonely

Nearby the prairie green

An Aria for the Dreary

Sung in the heart of spring

A chorus of world weariness!

At where these shadows play

Blue skies corrupt in cloudiness

Above the evening day

1365

Oh, to be kissed by the elite

Is such a desired thing

Whether or not its genuine

Is to no consequence

Oh, the sweet smell of success

Sings hearty in my head

Kisses from the worthy elite

Before I'm left for dead

Jonathan Lovejoy

1366

Lately, I find myself alone

A ghost adrift

Left to languish on my own

Unjoyful gift

1367

Beauty chicks serve market fellow

And now there'll be time to lay

Cracked on the rock of prosperity

Waiting to be born

On the morning after waiting

A sharp pain cries forlorn

Though a spirit lies in shambles

Wrinkled, tattered and torn

Travelers return--a weary trip

Thoughts unbridled are made to slip

Of what sibling wished to let 'er rip

"Your husband's madness!" born

306th Assembly

1368

Don't like it—don't try it!

Don't mike it—don't deny it!

The journey of the prairie queen

Don't strike it—don't fry it

Don't spike it, don't dry it

A trip shot like arrows in the spleen!

1369

The trip is over for the night queen

And her prince along for the ride

A flight through rain and misery

'Til there be nowhere left to hide

1370

Ambiguity is obsolete

Though it be tried and true

A touch of mystery can't be beat

The Queen of Amherst knew

The soul of the poet is shrouded

By Ambiguity

1371

What form lust and vanity doth take?

Young innocence—female

Driven to disrobe

To paint the face

To smile--

To dance with fever

What form--lust and vanity!

Beauty expressed through the dance!

Dressed to allure the eyes--

From innocence

307th Assembly

1372

We strive as unto the Lord

For perfection

Then we jive as unto God—

For protection

To be shielded from the cold Hand of Judgment

That will yield fire upon our skin

Stay thy hand of discipline, O Lord!

We beseech thee, Heavenly Father—

For our righteousness

Is as filthy rags before thee!

So we beg thy pardon, O God

That our perfection is imperfection itself—

That we have no hope of pleasing thee!

1373

*H*aving thought our friendship was real
Unprepared for what lay revealed
The day I came to call

Among the worldly goods—
I saw her at play like a creature—
In the Forest Wood

In happiness I strolled to her
Asking "which thing do you prefer?"
As concerning what we knew

I watched her fade to whitened ice
A crystal blade--made fit to slice
My unbroken soul in two

1374

Woman, thou art a goddess

Skin of ivory cream

These, thine attending ladies

But no less lovely than thee

Eyes, the color of thine hair

Black as silken midnight

Cheeks touched by the Rose

To echo lips of crimson

1375

Knowledge hiding in the woods—

Bears no song for me.

Crushing all my hopes to naught,

Though all I want is little—

Knowledge enjoys his woodsy space

Or his bright place in the sun,

Chirping platitudes like the bird

Until the day is done.

Knowledge enjoys his privelege

Reknowned to every hamlet—

Smiling foolishness from sea to shore

Because I can't get in—

Jonathan Lovejoy

308th Assembly

Jonathan Lovejoy

1376

My pillow is my briefcase
My office chair—my bed
My linen is my workstation
To sleep the sleep of the dead

Days lost—
Nights gamboled away
Where folly is to dream
Connections made—
Where thoughts will fade—
Where Destiny's labour is done

Elizabethan X

1377

Friends from many a year before

Cloaked in purple and fine linen

Do flounder upon the world stage

When their Destiny comes to call

Those who shouldn't open their mouths

To speak so wildly out of turn

Dimwittedness or a death wish

Causes stupidity to burn

A stubborn witch is in the floor!

Buried up to her skinny head—

Asking that it be kicked away

'Til her headless body—

Is dead

1378

When winter woods have gone away

Their cloak of green is warm

Whispers kissed by sunny breezes

Envious Matterhorn!

Nature dies a winter's sleep

By every year--forlorn

Dying their summer cloaks away

When Autumn winds are born

1379

Alien visitors in the night
On the eve of a crisis in oil
Prices fluctuating wildly—
While men weep and howl over riches spoiled

Alien visitors in the night
On the eve of a crisis in drugs
Men and women on the junkman's itch
While attempts to make them clean have failed

Alien vistors in the night
On the eve of a crisis in war...

1380

The lowly tulip—

But a weed at the Gates of Heaven

Beauty in our feeble sight

An echo of the Garden

309^{thh} Assembly

1381

Awake! Thy fragile nerves, awake!
To see what hath transpired
Gaze the darkened window pane—
What madness hath conspired!

What demon rips the wood away—
Leaves the glass unbroken?
As to what black magic this be
Unshattered glass in revelry—
Awake! Thy fragile nerves and see—
Clarity--unspoken!

Gaze the unwooded window pane
A window to the soul
Decrescendo thy spirit fear
To sanity—thy goal

A heart hath raced so far and near—
Demons empty the wood!
Unfetter my spirit's Night Scream—
Death to the Heart of Good!

1382

As to the spitting cobra

Whose saliva is not water

An open mouth—from a distance

Is acid for the eye

As to Katrina's Victims

Whose salvation was not water

Help! Come quickly, they said

Its not a black thing—

Its an American thing!

Jonathan Lovejoy

1383

One night, I pushed the veil of fear
When April's warm was on
Stepped into the earthen shadow
Azalia's Pink was gone

Onto the porch—a deadly stroll
My look above the pines
Attention drawn to the night field
Where wept—and will it find?

I looked away the prairie green
My look! Stolen another way!
Down the street toward Civilize
A trembling nerve in brief disguise--
Desiring bravery

Ev'ry star--a pinpoint in the sky
Why must I search to care?
Lights upon a black'ned sheen
My heart is fading there

Elizabethan X

Another glance—their chariots

In Ardmore Village Park

Blue stars descended upon them

Unmoving in the dark

1384

Money is a stream of water
My hands, a cracked wood pail
'Cept I be blessed to seal the hole
'Twill be my right to fail

Money! Money! A siphon chord
Plugged tight into the wall
Energy from my feeble mind
'Til "Breakdown" comes to call

It is the root of all evil—
The love of it—they say
But trying to live without it—
Carries a price to pay!

310th Assembly

1385

A slow, southern style
Is the only way to be--
Busy bees, forest trees
Summer breeze
Life of ease
Whistling council of the bird
Take your leisure—as you please!
Rest, Southern Style!

1386

Oh, to breathe fresh air unfettered

How I miss the sun!

Shaded by the Flowering Tree

'Til the final race is won

1387

Apollo at the Western Gate
In grieving to rush in
Painting the clouds in amber--
Thoughts of what might have been

Take my hand, Precious Lord!
Save me from the evil eye
Hearts of those who wish me harm--
Fallen from the sky

1388

Across the nighttime horizon

Every star speaks a tune

To offer me a consolation

Until the chariot's light is born

Apollo at the Eastern Gate

To light the Monday morn

On the day's journey to Aurora

The eastern clouds adorned

Jonathan Lovejoy

311th Assembly

Jonathan Lovejoy

1389

*S*wishing trees! Driving rain!

April sun is banished again

Trees bow down the heavy wind

Crushed to agony

April showers in the Garden

Driven in the breeze

Stormy wrath of springtime

Forest trees—beware!

A cloud adrift--not idling by

Threatening to swirl

Whirling gales beneath the gray

Still crashing waves in Melancholy Bay

Showers fall—do tempest rest?

Azalia's Pink in jest!

Showers drift the mighty clouds

Crest at Flower's Canyon

1390

Aspirations die a slow death

In the grieving land

The name appears ineffectively

On the cover of the blue

A visit from the non-elite

Chattering of donations

Believing she is a worthy cause

Unable to see the truth

Run! Run through the darkened streets!

Run from your destiny!

It calls your name loud enough for the dead to hear

To capture you in the rain

Jonathan Lovejoy

1391

Melodies from the 3rd heaven
Bestowed upon us all
Nom—again—music in the Hall
To train a beast of burden

Don't go "Guinivere"—there's no need
There's still more bread to leaven
Though we sing melodies from above
At the door of Apocalypse

Feeding frenzy at the zoo
When instincts come to call
A poet would rather wither and die
Than be on display at all

From Death comes Redemption
A reprieve from this prison ward
For to be absent from the body
Is to be present with the Lord

1392

The wind blows over yonder

Waiting for me

The end of days to ponder

So patiently

Jonathan Lovejoy

1393

The stormy sea of emotion
Blows casually away
A threat to sanity—nothing more
Knocking violently at my door

Billowing, swirling twisters observed
Underneath a clear blue sky
Looking, feeling, sounding deadly
Unable to sustain

Unable to maintain—
What had come just before
The lightning hailstorms—
The violent wind—
Threatening to blow down my door

But *only this*—
And nothing more

312th Assembly

Jonathan Lovejoy

1394

Let us cease the pretty talk

Of what constitutes a life

Suffer the unjust rain—

Live and die in vain

Some are born under a cloud

A storm of fervent pain

The robin be damned

And crushed under foot

As I live and die—

In vain

1395

From Antiquity to the present
The Crown Prince keeps me
In times of sorrow
Which hath nobly been—

From sunup to sundown
Each day of the millineum
In this new century,
Though the years have passed,

His spark hath not diminished
That lightning—
That thunderous chorus of ingenuity
The joyous crescendo

The inexhaustible Well of Inspiration
Invention,
Spontaneity,
Melodies from the God and the King

Clowned upon—
By The Crown Prince
To see me through the storm

1396

*T*reachery blows a warning

In the storm of a rising wind

Upon the rooftop of danger lies

Threatening to fall

Ghosts scream in revelation--

"You'll be broken if you drop!

Take heed the knife—on the burning tin—

And come to a sudden stop!"

1397

If I ever threw a party
I know no one would come
'Tis not a thing to worry on
It is the way for some

Turn thy loneliness unto Him
And pray thy sorest need
Savour your precious time alone
When you're untouched by them

The words appear as Autumn Leaves
Drying up in the Sun
Lost at the feet of The Lonely
Accompanied by none

313th Assembly

1398

A visit to the doctor—tally ho!

The purpose of your life—

Valley ho!

Confirmation—your birth is a joke—

And the joke is on you, don't you know!

Ask! Ask! Ask Heaven for a reprieve—

See what you get!

Does it matter at all what you believe?

You bet! What you get, you'll regret!

But don't let it cause you a fret

Your future is set—

So take what you can get

And die well

The farmer in the dell—The farmer in the dell—

Hi ho the derry-o

The farmer in the dell!

The farmer fell off the old tin roof

And broke both legs?

Oh, well!

1399

*H*aunted by my own blood—
Threatening to kill
Coursing deadly through my veins
With independent will

Jonathan Lovejoy

1400

The seed with severed regret—
There might be a summer upon this
How it has come to claim thee
I will never know

A broken cistern in the alley!
If you watch your step—there'll be no blood
Now, touch the cement and bricks to your soul
And flee the city, while you can!

There's gold in them there hills!
Nuggets of peace and safety
The fireball won't even get you
'Til the city is melted first—

The trees will light like matches
On that Great and Terrible Day!

313th Assembly

Jonathan Lovejoy

1401

Through labour and leisure

Laughter and lamentation

He keeps me whole—

Cast all thy worries at his feet

Then live as unto Him

For how much strength of worry is required?

To change the course of a mighty river?

Upon this River of Fate, we ride

To the Sea of Destiny

Sleep thy course—

Until thou art awakened

At the end of our long journey—

To the Sea

1402

Two robins—sent to comfort me
What are they but a sign?
That this is not the land before
But a new abode in time

Two trees--at home where they do live
White blossoms in the spring
Flourish nearby the prairie green
Wildflower's Pink between

1403

When "Papageno" comes to call

Sing the melody in swing time

To enliven the classroom of your life

Helping you to learn

While others share enthusiasm

In the Learning Hall

Search the wire for the Palace of Perversion

Threatening to burn

From Paris 1829

The final answer is earned

Five hundred times in the lifeline

Of melodies to turn

1404

*L*ook closely at the pieces

That are already done

To see what path embarked upon—

If it be the chosen one

314th Assembly

1405

The purple testament is on

It sings a lullabye

To lull my sensibilities

Away from Hope of Good

It rings!

It sings!

1406

Beauty pays an unwelcome visit
To the cottage by the sea
The caretaker says—"blow her a kiss"
In a flight of profound ignorance

A ghost wafts nearby
Unhinging a fragile nerve
In the wake of old demon lies
That the blessing is too small

Mongolian walks in humiliation
Looked upon negatively
Hoping for a greater reprieve
In the cottage by the sea

1407

Number Zero is a hero—
Nearer, O God, to thee!

Number One is fun
As daytime in the sun
Number Two is true
A friend to me and you

Number Three is me
Under the Flowering Tree
Number Four is more
Waiting at my door—

Zero is a hero—
Nearer, O God, to thee!

Number Five is alive
Helping happiness survive
Number Six is a mix
Of laughter and tricks

Elizabethan X

Number Seven is heaven
With friendships to leaven
Number Eight is great
At Prairie Green Estate
Number Nine is fine
For joyful hearts divine—

But Zero is a hero—
Nearer, O God, to thee!

Jonathan Lovejoy

1408

On the eve of disillusionment

In the morning of spring

Birds chirp my unholy demise

With a new and solemn song to sing

The ancestry lurks the Halls of Learning

Looking for a soul to kill

"You'll do 90 days" she says

In a proclamation of doom

Poverty mothers work in the breeze

With no hope for tomorrow

Fluttering the winds of change

Where "Sarah Girl" awaits

The progeny runs a hoop dream

Ineffectively

In the School of Politics and Prophecy

And promise of desire

315th Assembly

Jonathan Lovejoy

1409

The violin sings a happy tune
A poignant melody in the breeze
Intertwined by the Trio of Violence
Inside the Cage of Reason

The happy melody converts to sorrow
'Twined by the Trio of Lost Hope
Mourning for days of violence coming
When the cello steals the song—

Cadenza offers a revelation
Extended to infinity
In the quartet for "Noah's Ark"
On the eve of Armageddon

1410

From the grave, I sing this song. It was my place for hiding in…
They held me prisoner, right or wrong? It was a place called *Gunga Din.*
Grandmother's mansion house I knew, a palace golden through and through
Beside where the Kipling Forest grew, our privileged place for hiding in

Now, from the grave, I sing this song—of depravity hidden and family sin
In nineteen hundred and ninety two, dear Mother's heart was born in two
Torn asunder by what she knew—our place for hiding in—
Grandmother's youthful beauty true, the soul of what she had to do
To torment her daughter's body through! Pervertedness and blue.

One night, the Spirits spoke in turn, when Grandmother's daughter chose to run
In Mother's heart, her freedom burned, for refuge in the Sun
These selfsame Spirits spoke with ease, to capture mother in the room—
Grandmother's daughter shackled to the bed—a prisoner of Doom
Grandmother tortured her to fright, in ways that cannot be assumed
In Luna's journey across the Night, Mother's grief resumed

Weakling Kitten sister dear, in aid to assist Grandmother's blood
My Sister held my Mother tight, transmogrified to Mud
Hope transmogrified to Mud, while faith was dipped in blood
Grandmother tortured her daughter to death, in linen stained with blood!

Jonathan Lovejoy

From the grave, I sing this song! It was my place for hiding in—
In the palace by the Kipling Wood—it was a place called *Gunga Din*

In fervent strife—I braved the call—from Grandmother's mighty mansion inn
Oh, what fleet of foot I fly, to the palace by the Kipling Wood!
To take residence in the Golden Room, where Mother's grief had stood
Aged Beauty and Weakling Kitten, at the grave we prayed the common good
They tell me Mother's heart was smitten, as a widow's grieving should—

Now, take your rightful place with us, begs Grandmother Angelinari's tone
As I, Sarah Girl, gaze on her Beauty, in awe of what is known—
For Lust and Vanity and Pride—I kill the simple life I own!
In the palace where my Mother died—my Grandmother and Sister's Home!
From the grave, I sing this song—it was my place for hiding in
In the Mansion by the Forest Wood—compelled to remember when

One night, I was visited in my bed—nearby the moonlit Summer Wood
There are things that I need to do, she said, *things that your mother understood*
If I am to have my youth and beauty, there are necessities to control
By the Spirits, I do my solemn duty, to feed upon your Soul.
This, by tortures unimagined, by depravities you have never known
Burning the Angelinari Blood—to even thy sister, these Spirits shown
Suffer what you must endure, accept what punishments must be
Surrender for pleasure thy pains allure—Spirits! Her Body and Soul to Thee!
Otherworldly and unknown Desire, to imprison and torture my soul between!
Days come and go—as do the seasons—In the palace I was hiding in
Now from the grave, I sing this song—nearby the Mansion called *Gunga Din*

Elizabethan X

Seven generations, the curse of God! Behind closed doors and sin
By the Spirits I wept in blood and pain, in the mansion house where I was in
These shackles can be done away, accept thy pain and live
Just say the word, I heard Grandmother say, *or there'll be no more mercy to give*
Epiphany! I nod my head—surrender to the pain!
Lightning screams Truth to the buried dead—reprieve falls by the Summer Rain
The leather leaves where my arms had bled—how can I move again!
On what wind hath Sanity fled, from where I was hiding in!

A body broken—trembling fear, waiting for their return
Knowing what sister said was clear—*tonight, she must be burned!*
By the Spirits—their solemn demand, when a heart has given in
My back must bear the burning brand! Blistered upon my skin!
My back must bear the burning brand—O, where doth fear begin!
O, carry me now, to another Land, to a place I've never been!
I hear the Ghost of the Kipling Wood—moaning of my defeat
"East is East, and West is West, and never the twain shall meet!"

I hear the creak of the Mansion Door, footsteps from in the Hall
To sound my demise over the Mansion Floor, I grieve what sufferings befall!
Grandmother Angelinari—Sister Dear—standing in my room
What truth is told in the lightning storm—this Firebrand of Doom!
Weakling Kitten—Lioness—adrift as in a dream
Away, I pull! A madwoman possessed—in the lift of my hallowed scream!
Sweet promises—bare thy soft caress! For my screaming to decrescend—
Oh, How I have longed—I must confess—Of how my life came to end!

I break away—their evil kiss, to shriek this last crescendo—

To the outstretched arms of Freedom—I run—and crash through the mansion window!

I fall—through the cold summer rain, I fall—in Freedom's lovely flight

To take the hands of palace brick below, in the storm of a Summer's Night

Now from the grave, I sing this song! Of the prison where I was hiding in

Of how I arrived in my coffin bed, by the Palace of *Gunga Din!*

1411

A lash of pain is a memory
Somewhere along the line
Another reason to regret--
Living

A memory is a lash of pain
Inside the flow of time
Another reason to despair--
This life

A pain is a lash of memory
Within the paradigm

1412

$\mathscr{B}$eauty is Power—

Enjoy it if you have it

It is a gift from God

Money is Power—

Enjoy it if you have it

It is a gift from God

316th Assembly

1413

Across a northern highway
Is ingenuity wrought through skill
In the haze of mist and fog
Majesty can be seen—

What's happening on the eastern highway?
What miraculous consequential thing—
Can compare to what rises above it?
Still captured by the snow

Across the horizon, east to west
Along the northern road
Lies the Appalachian mountain peak
Across the Northern Line

Thing of beauty—so special!
Risen above the natural world—
In unnatural splendor

1414

The Voice of God is loud and clear
When heard through the bars of music
Melodies of Kelly Green
Irish through and through

The flute carries my soul to Heaven
Raptured by the strings
Echoed of the English horn
Captured by the spring

The Voice proclaims—the tomb is empty!
Good news left to tell
To those in fear instead of living life
Who know pain and suffering so well

The Voice of God in the bars of music!
Oh, blessed assurance divine—
Carried aloft on the Golden Horn
In victory, Jesus is mine

1415

*W*hen a flower's welcome is worn

There is no real regret

As surely as it came and died

Another one you'll get

1416

Ambition is the heart of boredom

Restlessness galore

Killing desires unfulfilled

Answers never born

317th Assembly

1417

*T*he family man lived a good life
Then, he died a good death
His spirit roamed across the farm
After his final breath

The farmhouse he had made was swept
His land was lush and green
The cornfields were fit for harvest
With nothing in between

"I had them all fooled" his ghost said
Imprisoned by the door
But instead of through the ceiling—
His ghost fell through the floor!

Something bad's going to happen—
To this impacted soul
Laid in Womack Cemetery
His ghost gone down to *Sheoul*

1418

Voices carry in the wind

To be heard by those who shouldn't

Family trials and tribulations

Swirling in the wind

Days of suffering bestowed

To eat a body away

Condemning a soul to a dark path

To where the promise is known

1419

She torments my heart with beauty

'Til I am broken

Burdened by the need to express

The unspoken word

Emily! Emily!

My dearest heart to thee!

Beg thy pardon—bear no contempt—

For me

From here--to eternity with thee—

I pine—

Inadequately

1420

When every flower hath corrupted

One doth still remain

To reminisce of a better peace

And prosperity

Then this flower dieth still

And withers quiet away

318th Assembly

1412

There is no further life for me

Outside my bonny bay

A prisoner of the journey

Across a rainy day

From these clouds pour my redemption

The course I dream--to stay

By the dreary revelation

Of my appointed way

When her name glows the blocks of light

Perserverance driven

Until history bears her name

Suffering is given

1413

The cracking Earth—

Split the sky in two

Burn the rain with fire

Blue sparks—

A river in the clouds

Dis Tracting my desire

1414

To approach the end of Maya's Call

Sanity in sight

At last, foolishness put away

So His Will is done

The level of stupidness—insurmount

Caromed from the hills

Conclusion—confusion—delusion

No amount of skill

1415

Inspiration is so fused with sales

That no man can measure

All of it from the throne of God

Whereby His teachings lie

Jonathan Lovejoy

319th Assembly

1416

Aqua green and marmalade trim
Set in the field of white
Woven upon the harvest loom
In the throes of winter spite

Protection from a falling rain
Our journey toward the night
Untold prosperity awaits
Much so--my soul's delight

Detour in the amaranthine
Awashed their woes of might
While I gather my blessings due
A spirit posed contrite

1417

The new breed of churches

Is Laodicea

Which will honor Him with their lips

But their hearts are far from Him

With every corruptible seed

And every good work

Having a form of Godliness

Denying the power thereof

In the Laodicean church

Worldliness is king

Association by evil--

And every wicked thing

1418

I like you well enough

But I can't stand the children

The modern refrain of games

Played with their young lives

Pretending to be so in love with the children

Through the impending divorce

As they are mere pawns in a game

Because they are hated

1419

Church of Laodicea

Who shall pay for thy wrongdoing!
The children shall reap the rewards
For thy sin

We are rich! Increased with goods!
Our hearts are far from him
Lift thy head from thine shoulders—
Laodicea!
Accept what thou dost deserve!

Jonathan Lovejoy

320th Assembly

1420

I can feel you taking me, Lord

Was the father's refrain

As he lay dying on the floor

Poisoned by the pain

1421

Daisies in the lily field!
Lilies in the daisy field—
Cornflowers blue—
Yellow daffodils do sing!

Dandelions prepare their truth—
To carry upon the wind
Grasslands blow—
This selfsame breeze—
In waves—
The wildflower field

Stalks of grass--dipped
Tipped in gold or white
Golden rises—
Fluttering the breeze

To fly in memory—
Across the prairie field

1422

In the ceiling fan man, I see—
Five heads looking at me
Though there be only one

Identical to every arm
Likewise to every leg
For his descenscion in my sleep
To run across the floor

Elizabethan X

1423

Monsters roll the streets

Of my abode

Swooping above and below—

Nearby the prairie green

Demons patrol the paths

Of my kingdom

Hearing the call of the whisper

When I open my door

But the window overlooks the prairie field

Safe from eyes that stare

Jonathan Lovejoy

321st Assembly

1424

I saw a blackbird in the grass
He wandered to and fro
When he was done, he took his flight
To where, I'll never know

I heard a blackbird in the trees
Laughing a call at me
When he was done—he flew again
To where, I'll never see

I saw a blackbird in the sky
He flew so far away
When he was done, he stopped to rest
To where, I cannot say!

1425

Oceans upon the floor

Breeding sharks--therin

Run! Swim away from them!

Lest their feasting begin

"Debilitating," they are

I heard the demon say

Haunted by the poisoned blood

When dark turns into day

1426

Hear the voice in the whispering wind
A message from above
Love—and Joy—and Peace—and Mercy
Descending like a dove

Hear nature in the rising wind
What river of breezes flowing!
Whispered eschatology—
In gentle breezes blowing

Like waves upon the grain
In ripples through the field

1427

Imagine a gust of wind—
With strength to rip a house apart
In but a second—
And carry the debris away?

What is a funnel cloude?
What is the gale of a hurricane—
If not the almighty power of God?

Study thy mansion home—
Lovely brick by brick
And know that their strength is as glass
To the whirlwind

Their power is that of a wafer
They are as heavy as the lightest feather—
In the cloude

Elizabethan X

322nd Assembly

322nd Assembly

1428

Chased by red and white lights

The death chariot rides

Whirling white—siren

Crimson in the gray—

In the palace lot of learning—

Beg the choke of death—stop!

Let me live!

Take me no more by the neck

To draw breath from me

Do not pull my arm—

To throw me in the chariot

When the crimson light—

In the gray—

Comes for me

1429

Messages written in thine own blood

Fret not—"The Doctor" is in

To inquire whether a sport was played

To carry the beast within—

By genius—likewise was him

Stifled by the mother line

Dismantled—brick by brick

Made to know the darker side of life

To carry the beast within—

By genius—likewise was him

A mighty hand around thy neck

Both tall in cut and grass'

In thine own blood—messages appear

To carry the beast within—

By genius—likewise by him

A tomb

Jonathan Lovejoy

1430

Recruit to a higher calling

Will cause a sudden change

A cutting down to smaller size

So new growth may arrange

A period of transition

And wasted energy

A struggling amateur

Just before it is meant to be

Every tree is known by its fruit

In summoned forth due time

While the leaves suffer in waiting

Their sweetest paradigm

323rd Assembly

Jonathan Lovejoy

1431

Even with wax and clay figures—
They don't move as much as they used to
Hours of repined, refined regret—
Still knocking at the door

What kind of wisdom is this—
That steals your heart away?
Bubble gum beauty is tried and true
But perhaps is not for you

Having ridden all the waves—
Hidden from the truth—in lies
There lies the most ancient rub of all—
That schemes are done in passing

1432

*B*uried in perpetuity

A demon, in the room

Houses of utter destruction

Crumbling in the blue

Blackbirds flock to kill

Outside the home of perpetuity

While I roam around inside

Imprisoned by the curtain

Best friends in the evening day

Tend to go their separate ways

Except diplomacy intervene

Persuading them to stay

In the halls of prosperity

Future perpetuity

Problems lurk on every wall

Passing through the mother line

Layers of decoration

In every generation

Hiding what the walls have seen

Across the grandest nation

1433

Five hundred bounce and heeble head
Heeble, hobble-headed green
Wee wobble ween, and Wilcomb Lean
Wip Willam Willy womp Wilson

Tie the chickens to the beams, baby
Let 'em dangle—
The assembly line carries the truth in skin
Cause no matter how hard you try, big boy—
Success and Prosper ain't gon' let you in!

Warm your cold hands by the furnace
The stars are out at night
Though the furnace is red hot with power
The iron is cracked—erudite

Find a way to kill yourself
You ain't gon' never get in!

Elizabethan X

The curse of God flows the mother line
Listen to me, blubber boy—SIN!

Wait by the railroad tracks, Slim Jim—
For a train that ain't comin' again
Find a way to kill yourself, Willy Bill—
Your momma should have done it when you were TEN!

Jonathan Lovejoy

1434

Spider Man has tossed the hat
With no more life to give
Auntie May has bossed the cat—
With no more life to live!

Bubble gumdrop doilies—
Foibles in the twilight breeze—
Noises from the busy bees
Buzzing their life of ease

Blanche won't reminisce—
About the days she spent in Sook
Rose won't reminisce
About the lies her daughter took—

To tell her—Mom, you're not going to Hell
Your ridiculous life is swell
So what if you're in the hospital—
The farmer is in the Dell!

Elizabethan X

Calling up to pack his bags—
Lucipher is up from the well!

Jonathan Lovejoy

324th Assembly

1435

Gioacchino Rossini at the piano
To display a proper flair
Melodies from out of nowhere
Conjured from the air

Flashpoint! Magic on the keys!
In Antonio Amadeus form
Lightning! Bestowed upon the Italian
To conjure up a storm

Vivaldi! Mozart! Rossini!
The skies bear homage to thee!
In icy hail and blue energy—
Whirlwind's Majesty

1436

Lost the lamp shades in every hue—

Alabaster white to Ocean blue

Made of satin—silken jade

To soft lit every plan was laid

In misery—for what he had to do

Cruising throughout the rainy day

Still looking for the shade—

While Money Man observes--disappointedly

Restrained—abstaining—

In the rain

1437

The Four Winds of Womanhood are these:

Eyes—

Lips—

Breasts—

Hips—

Oops! Did I let it slip?

Savour thy slim waisted—curve waisted trip

Across the Four Winds of Womanhood

1438

*T*he antisocial busy bee
I never meant to be
Studying was my only path
To immortality

A highway I should have taken
Though too afraid to try
Too dark and difficult a road
I wished to travel by

The antisocial busy bee
I willingly agree!
Buzzing every flower alone—
A pencil pedigree

Jonathan Lovejoy

325th Assembly

1439

Three bear witness to "Idols"
And yet, these three are one
Thy light to guide these flailing youth—
Knowledge, Wisdom, and Truth

1440

A prisoner of the clergy
Their whim and will
Taking what they throw my way
With fervent skill

The line to sustenance is long
A wilderness
Mocked by those who wait no more
Tempers rising

A test for when to hold the tongue
Flung through the air
In the confines of my prison line
Burned cakes are thrown

Almaviva haunts the poverty line—
Rosina's Home

Jonathan Lovejoy

1441

Place the book on the keys—

Play the song with ease

Do it quickly, lest you forget—

And fall down weak in the knees

Two stood at the piano board—

To educate the least of these!

But when he relayed what they had played

No sound would stay from the keys!

1442

Plastic money is a golden cage

Guilded on borrowed treasure

A cycle of death and debt resumes

Until all life is gone

Those who live in the Golden Cage

Succomb because of greed

Given over to materialism

And things they'll never need

Plastic money is Debtor's Prison

For the naïve and the simple

A cage built by Lust and Vanity

Inhabited by greed

Climbing high into the sky—

Threatening to pop!

The Golden Cage is on a bubble

Rising to the top

Jonathan Lovejoy

326th Assembly

1443

*D*aytime stars glisten in the trees

To visit a chosen few

Sparkling in the rising sun

Upon the morning dew

His message shines every starlight

Day or Nighting Time

Across the morning Son—and the heavens

Along the evening line

1444

*T*he essence of the ram is jade

Shrank to emerald light

On the eve before the final journey

Appearing as a ring

Clouds coalesce and fall again

To drown a wayward soul

Lying in the mud, in a rainstorm

Nearby the sleep of death

I carry the dead soul to medicine

What level of thanks will his mother give?

Needles emerge from nowhere

To prick a heart to blood

1445

An angel is on your shoulder
Guiding you through life
Pointing the way through pitfalls
Those unclearly seen

When eyes awake in safety
The Guardian was there
Staying the hands of Death and Destruction
Unbeknownst to thee

Bad haircuts and boyfriends—
Destiny—nonetheless
Good haircuts and girlfriends—
By the Will of God

1446

On my stroll with the Playmaker
Along the trail to Nowhere
Blue cloth decorates ambition
To commemorate our arrival

The Playmaker and the Prophet
At the foot of the world stage
One having lived and died already—
The other—grieving to get in

Jonathan Lovejoy

1447

Stars in the field of midnight
In the bands of crimson white—
"Oh, say can you see"—the poet writes
Near *"by the Dawn's early light"*

Our colors of freedom ride the wind
By her Glory we wish to fight—
"Oh say can you see"—the poet writes
Near *"by the Dawn's early light"*

The banner unfurls the Winds of Time
Uncurled over the Tide of Right
"Oh, say can you see"—the poet writes
Near *"by the Dawn's early light"*

Seventeen seventy six is home
A beacon—to guide us through the night
"Oh, say can you see"—the poet writes
Near *"by the Dawn's early light"*

327th Assembly

1448

That insanity that hit—

Must've been it

'Cause I took another look at those chapters—

And they fit!

1449

Those that see me

See the living dead

Adrift in and out of my room—

Near my grieving bed

Jonathan Lovejoy

1450

No mountain of success
May shadow peace of mind
Duress howls the nighttime—
Nearby the Paddling Wood

A child burdened by stress
Under the ancestry
Crushed by the hand of pain
On the chariot wheel

There can be no escape
From suffering meant to be
A cross for them to bear
By Destiny's Decree

1451

*A*raven haired with naught to do
Brightened by what she ought to do—

1452

*H*ell on one side—

Paradise, the other

On one side—

There lies a grassland

A prairie field of flowers—

Ocean blue—petals--

Companion of sunny yellow

And snowy white—

Bowing to warm summer winds—

Touched by cooling breezes that blow

Alongside the Prairie Field—

Resides the line of Forest Green—

Where the Prairie breeze goes—

When it flows a song of peace—

Whispered prosperity upon the leaves

Above the Forest Green,

There rises the flower blue—

The ocean that is sky,

To a horizon unseen—

Elizabethan X

Brushed by the color of Lilies from the Field—

In clouds of fluffy, snowy white

on the other side—

i hear the vOiCe of *hammering* mEtAl—

the roar of smoke and eNgine noise—

vOices joined by yells and calling words—

the clamour oF *avarice*—

the scream oF *ambition*—

the stench of *pride*—

arrogance in agony and soot—

laughter, blackenIng the sky—

to coalesce in charcoal clouds,

fire and vapouR of smoke—

a fervent heat of choking—

poisonous—

dEath and *dying*

Jonathan Lovejoy

328th Assembly

1453

*B*alletic skill at what you do
Is beauty to behold
Whether clocking the hands of time
To necromance a rhyme--

Even to don a boxing glove
With talent from above
Perhaps to catch a football throw
By love of elegance

So pay attention to the signs
What truth bestowed from them
Extraordinary ability--
Is evidence of Him

"Touch not mine anointed," he says
A message from the hill
Hear from their beauty--to behold
Songs of balletic skill

1454

"*Y*ou're always welcome in my heart"
The boy heard in the line
With the yellow-suited others
Marching to find a way

The Prophet shrinks down to Beauty
In alabaster cloth
To prophecy inspiration
Bestowed from up Above

The Players of Amadeus
In Glory to perform
The Players of Orchestra's Light
Defeated in the fight

1455

Close the door and rearrange
Where law and order just can't be
Cop a high and feed the "Strange"
And everything that's killing me

Laura Lee walks in the dark
Looking for a place to be
A ghost lives in Cemetery Park
Walking and waiting for me

You can take nothing from Eschatology
And the coming end of the world
Burning in my psychology--
A cemetery girl

1456

Scattered diligence in the dark

To impede a destination

Hunger coalesced in pink and white

To precede a celebration

329th Assembly

1457

The river of pain runs purple

Agony of Defeat

In the marble hall of dying

Away from the elite

One half removed from the third year

Of Eli's visit here

Gone is the Woman of the North

Flocked like a bird in fear

Muddy waters from the river

To flow a Crested Sea

While I wait for Defeat to come

Most inevitably

1458

God has no obligation

To our unworthy decree

Unanswered prayers—to our benefit

Unanswered foolishness

Lest we wish ourselves ragged—

To the bottom of the sea

God has an obligation

To his Divine Decree

That *"whosoever believeth in him*

Should not perish—

But have everlasting life"

1459

Place the wings back in the oven

They're not ready

Time to concern yourself with yo-yo girl

In her leather bikini

Soccer moms roll the streets

Causing us to look

Ruling the airways and the highways

With prettiness as the hook

She's busy! She's blonde! She's buxom!

What she does is a luxury to see!

In faded blue jeans and rose colored top

And irresistibility

1460

*T*ogether, we can work it out!

No matter that love has flown the coop!

T'was not love anyway—

But lust and romance—

And surface foolishness gone

1461

Grab the barking dog by the ears

And she will cease to bark

Then pray that she will run away

To avoid the killing blood

Inspiration is a fickle bird

Independence is golden

330th Assembly

1462

On the Campus of Fallen Leaves

Infidelity seeks to confound

Though the lips of another are warm and sweet

There are consequences to know

Though we climb aboard the rocket ride

Hoping for pleasures untold

We cruise along to nowhere fast

Seeing others along the way

"They're out for what they can get"

A guilty party says to me

While the ancestry rises corruption

In the chariot of broken dreams

Bearing on what heroes are worth

As we glide the Campus of Fallen Leaves

In and of themselves, they are worthless

Without the Hand of God

Elizabethan X

Rising, falling, helping, hurting
Along their chosen way
Crushing mortals under appreciation
For their fervent deeds

Chosen paths appear as right
Along the Road of Life
Leading to the Campus of Fallen Leaves
Where wayward dreams go to die

1463

*T*his is the media age—

T-R-I in the sky

*T*elevision—

*R*adio—

*I*nternet—

Bringing the noise

1464

*S*wim! Brave the waters of the thrashing, stormy sea!

Lift thy head and breathe—

See the silhouette—

Enlightened

Enlivened

Illuminated by the storm

What borders are these?

Upon what shores are these waves—

The crashing, stormy sea?

In the flickering clouds—

His voice grows dim—

The calming waters,

The mind of Him

That--to provide refuge in the storm—

An end to thine epic swim—

Across the stormy sea

Crawl the shores of this paradise—

In choking

Stumble to where the Golden Iris is grown—

At the edge of the stormy sea

1465

Opinions need not vary on

The flow of time will tell

Obsolescence is clearly seen

By those who know it well

All gatherers in the Dead Land

Must pick and choose a way

No patrons for the Archaic

Dust from another day

Sensual perversion will rule

Neccesitates the flow of time

Days of innocence--are shattered

Above the Evening Chime

Jonathan Lovejoy

331st Assembly

Jonathan Lovejoy

1466

Although beauty is relative

Ugliness is absolute

That of the heart and soul

And the mind

To catch another crying pain—

Is a worthy goal in life

Guage the mirror to see the truth

Of Vanity's decree

1467

*B*eside the dirt road to nowhere
The empty cropfield lies
And the mansion at Amherst Lake
Over the Prairie Green

I glide offsides the traveling road
For the improper thruway
Lying to the preacher and his wife
Of what we're going to do

Swooing, swaying back to the road
Looking for Pastor Stackhouse
Guilty for lies directly told
To the couple at Prairie Green

1468

*O*f such evil that we see—

Choosing not to believe

That *"those who take up the sword*

Shall perish by the sword"

With the saw blade of Death in hand

To dismembering their brother

Hypocrisy sings Soprano

In judgment of another

To prophecy of curses

For those that do the crime

Tony—Carmella—A.J.—Meadow—

In the Winds of Time

1469

White cotton pillows—

In ashen gray regret

Brushed below with melancholy

Over the prairie field

Speeding—intrepidly

To where their tears must be

To replenish the ground in sorrow

And painful memory

Jonathan Lovejoy

332nd Assembly

1470

$\mathcal{S}$eeing a dead horizon tree
Is no deterrant for me
Toward unfulfilled prophecy—
I flee

Betrayal by the ancestry--
Of what surprise should it be?
Toward unfulfilled prophecy—
I flee

Being driven to a straight jacket
Where they await patiently
Toward unfulfilled prophecy—
I flee

The road is laid with treachery
As far as the eye can see
Unanswered prayers in the tea leaves
Whispered divine Decree—

Elizabethan X

Dragging another century

Enchained of Destiny

Toward unfulfilled prophecy--

I flee

1471

*A*ghost ship in the night sky
Passing overhead
Obscuring the stars of heaven
By declaration of the dead

1472

George Ivory is dead!
George Ivory is dead!
Lord, God Almighty—
George Ivory is dead!

In the Martin County timeline—
In the town nearby the Wooded Pine
Michael Ivory wedded Love
In Beauty's heart divine

Bumblebee flowers—pink roses—white
Of kisses—honeymoon's delight
Blissful rendezvous in the night
Underneath the Summer Moon

The brother of Michael happened by
By matrimonial pride
A busty hug from the newest bride
By the Martin County Wood

George Ivory is dead!
George Ivory is dead!

Oh, sweet Lord o' mine—
George Ivory is dead!

O Williamston! Eastern town!
By the Roanoke River flow
Look to the coffin bed below—
George Ivory is dead!

Snowy blossoms--what breezes blow?
In the cooling of the Evening Day
With his brother's wife—George Ivory lay—
In the town by the Wooded Pine

Black hearted blade—what silver curses flew?
Of thine comeuppance overdue?
When blood was spilled in rendezvous—
By Beauty's eye divine

At *slicing!* A brother's soul in two!
Behold! Thy commandment—burning through!
The ivory metal in blood and hue—
Infidelity's killing blood

A mother's pain down to the bone
When her son lay dead in Beauty's view
Sliced by the metal of another son
On the eve of ivory stone

Elizabethan X

George Ivory is dead!
George Ivory is dead!
Oh my Lord, dear God Almighty—
George Ivory is dead!

Leaves of Cemetery Way
Above these newest flowers grew
His name is carved in perpetuity
On the marble of ivory stone

O Williamston! Eastern town!
By way of the Roanoke River bride
Thy town near the woods of life in time
A recompence of peace sublime

Jonathan Lovejoy

1473

The giant serpent devours a meal

In keeping with the times

The irresolution of a friendship

About to be swallowed whole

Rumblings—along the timeline—cause the serpent

To regurgitate a meal

Can the living dead lie in appreciation—

Of a reprieve from Hell?

Satan is an anaconda

Slithering the hour

Looking for souls to feed upon—

And bodies to devour

333rd Assembly

1474

Mr. and Mrs. Front, don't fret—
"My damage is to the soul"
Said the Devil as he honored Them—
Who achieved their worthy goal

You look good! You're rich! You've got it made!
But no attention to thy soul was paid
Reap the reward of every plan you laid—
Thine life as King and Queen

But thy soul—I shall require of thee!
No further need to pretend
Pack your bags and come with me—
Your days have come to an end!

1475

The angel tapped me on the shoulder

As though he really cared

But when I turned to look at him--

There was nobody there!

Jonathan Lovejoy

1476

I saw a note on a sweet drink—
Purporting to care, I think
But what I perceived was Apathy,
In the bars of the scribbler's ink

1477

There exists such a great gulf--
Between innocence and corruption
That children do not always understand
The adult's way of thinking

Just as the wayward adult
Is confounded by the child
Why it may have no genuine concern
For this endeavor or that

For what child wishes to smear makeup upon its face?
And parade themselves in gaudy attire?
Xcept it be presented and taught--
By an adult?

For what child wishes to organize in warfare?
To engage one another in killing?
The heart of corruption rages on
Upon the battlefields of war

To unknowingly draw the children in
To our Vortex of Being

334th Assembly

1478

Somebody stole my poem from me
Hidden in the petals of a rose
Clipt—carried shamelessly away
Where my prose shall wither and die

A thief, says the chirping bird
In jealousy's repose
Slipt by—before nighttime broke to day
And carried my poem away

1479

Tambling over covered rain—
Ambling over a forest brook.
Stillness over there.
Hair.

A yellow butterfly—
Fluttering in the air

1480

The church is your last hope, isn't it?
The cushioned Baptist benches
The smell of pine and gentility—
The look of the burgundy carpet at your tired feet

1481

The frantic, hopeless screams of condemned flesh

Burning—

Burdened with desire

Cursed with inability to satisfy it

Jonathan Lovejoy

335th Assembly

Jonathan Lovejoy

1482

I hear the voice of God in the thunder
The sound of his sorrow in the rain

In the lightning, I see—
The eyes of Wrath—
Unrestrained—
Contained in the skies above me

1483

Buildings quake—

Rumbling…

Buildings shake,

Crumbling.

Jonathan Lovejoy

1484

O Lord, make me old--
And sleep me away.
He broke my heart,
And took my life away.

1485

Old shoes, new shoes

White shoes—

Blue shoes.

What does it all mean?

Jellybean.

Jonathan Lovejoy

336th Assembly

1486

Such a life so fragile
A scooter—pink.
Where monsters roar—
The path.

1487

Your back bears the memory of her love.

Fair skin tells of it

Her love is wrath—

Her wrath is beauty

Jonathan Lovejoy

1488

The tides of war are rising

Bullets—flown east to west

Addressed are issues—

Weighed heavy against every solder's life—

In desert moonlight—

Underneath the Summer Moon

Games are played,

Among the killing fields

Where the prize is Life—

Death flows the desert killing fields—

Underneath the Summer Moon

God-conscious of the Lady friend

Who befriends the soldier in battle--

She works her magic upon the Troop Man

To have his heart for she

She steals his heart and soul away—

In the dust of the eastern sea

Elizabethan X

The soldier rolls the moonlit night
Upon this rendezvous
To where his eastern girl awaits
There, in the light of the Summer Moon
The spirit of death awaits—
When her brothers pour from the shadows
In a haze of bullets and fire—
To see the western soldier dead
Underneath the Summer Moon

Oh, captain—my Captain!
In the light of the Desert Moon

Jonathan Lovejoy

1489

Curse the night—

Bless the day!

I'm going to feast,

In the east.

Later, beast.

1490

All forms of stupidity,

Pervade the night.

Night being the Fall of Man.

Wall.

Jonathan Lovejoy

337th Assembly

Jonathan Lovejoy

1491

A train through the tunnel—
Coldwater!
Never fear, there's beer.
Here.

1492

Strawberries, peaches and cream

You know that I love you, child.

Life dies in the handshake.

At Desert East.

Least.

1493

Unmade by human hands—

Unseen.

The brightest eye.

Spy.

1494

Where is your beloved daughter?

Where is the flower, born from your garden?

Where has the Rain Flower gone to rest?

338th Assembly

1495

The white bannister breaks—
A fall.
Tumbling through the air.
A broken neck.

Blood.

1496

Black cotton candy—

Tastes sweet.

So are things—

That are good to eat.

Money.

1497

*T*hank you—I'm ashamed of you
For being away so long
Where you've been, is sin again—
A question of Right and Wrong.

Now, get along.

339th Assembly

Jonathan Lovejoy

1498

She paints away the stress
Of a bleak tomorrow.
Her house is full of painted things.
And sorrow.

The man she wants—
Went to a neighbor's.
A blue spray can.
Labours.

1499

The fire in the walls—

Is out.

The explosion, he said—

Can't be put out…

The pain was in the pipes

Burning blue and black fire.

Ire.

1500

*W*ho knows—

If you have not found some place to have flown?
Some unknown country or another?

1501

At Failure's dark and distant shore
Bides the tide of reason
Protection from the mouth of Jaws
In this Lonely Season

A New World wilderness beckons
Under cover of night
In grieving for these sharks to slay
That swim my soul to bite

Having come back to the Dead Room
A grave--for me to live
Sticks of blue light my way to die—
A failure's life--to give

Jonathan Lovejoy

Elizabethan X

ABOUT THE AUTHOR

Jonathan Lovejoy is a graduate of the University of North Carolina at Greensboro, with a B.A. in Religious Studies. He currently lives in Winston Salem, North Carolina.

For more info on the author's life and career, visit jonathanlovejoy.com.